2022
AUSTIN
Restaurants

The Food Enthusiast's Long Weekend Guide

Andrew Delaplaine

*Andrew Delaplaine is the Food Enthusiast.
When he's not playing tennis,
he dines anonymously
at the Publisher's (considerable) expense.*

Senior Editor – James Cubby

Table of Contents

Introduction

Austin may always be one of those cities that people always have something to say about if they are familiar with it or have been there before, but it might never reach the top of their "Places I need to visit!" list.

However, if you do find yourself visiting the heart of Texas, you may be pleasantly surprised.

Who would have ever thought that engrained into the pulsing Republican, Conservative, and sometimes over-the-top Old Fashioned (we won't say racist) center of Texas is perhaps one of the most liberal and free spirited cities in the U.S.

I can't emphasize the importance of MUSIC in Austin. The **SXSW Festival** has energized the town and made it a center of music recognized around the world.

There is so much to see tucked amid all the natural beauty: smug latte drinkers at coffee shops, long-haired college students, struggling musicians (and not so "struggling"), corporate big heads (and their headquarters) all peacefully sequestered away in the rolling hills of Travis County just on the eastern part of the hill country of Central Texas.

This, ladies and gentlemen, is Austin!

<u>WATERLOO & THE BEGINNING</u>

The area around the Colorado River that Austin is hinged on has been inhabited by humans for an estimated 11,000 years at least (this is long before "Dazed and Confused" debuted).

Originally the Clovis Indians are known for dominating this area, with a few other tribes that passed through.

Texas won its independence in 1835-36 from Mexico and became its own country known as the Republic of Texas. Newly formed, Texas began looking for a place to call their capital. They were attracted to an area known as Waterloo as it provided grounds for a stable settlement. There were hills, fresh soil, and a river running through it. It was also a geographical center-point for trade routes between Galveston and Santa Fe. Travis County was established in 1840, and after some short altercations with a few Comanche Indians, settlement began.

Initially Austin grew very quickly, and of course met with a few setbacks including the heat from political giant Sam Houston who was disgusted with the formation of Austin as the Texas Capital. And of course, there was the Civil War.

GETTING ABOUT

Some say that Austin is a "College Town." Don't let that mislead you. The famed University of Texas is just one of the many interesting sights in Austin.

Austin and the surrounding areas make up the fourth largest metropolitan area in Texas with about 850,000 citizens. Austin is pretty much in the center of Texas at the border of the hill country (that moves westward in Texas) and situated on the banks of the Colorado River. Austin is in the middle of three cities, Dallas to the north, Houston to the east southeast, and San Antonio to the south.

Austin is about 200 miles by road south from Dallas (Dallas has a population of 1.2 million, and ranks as third largest city in Texas).

Houston is east of Austin (and a little south) and can be reached by Highway 290.

Houston has a population of over 2 million making it the highest populated area in Texas.

San Antonio is 81 miles South (and a little west) of Austin. San Antonio has a population of about 1.3 million (making it the second most populated area in Texas).

If you're just landing, you are most likely in Austin-Bergstrom International Airport (ABIA). ABIA is located just southeast of Central Downtown.

Central Downtown is where you will find most of your Entertainment and Dining, along with the famed University of Texas Campus. Central Downtown has many live music venues, fine dining (and some not so much), hotels, condominiums, Whole Foods Headquarters, and the State Capitol.

Recent construction has made it possible for travelers to access the airport without sitting in traffic in downtown.

The main highway that goes north and south through downtown Austin is Highway 35. During rush hour traffic this is a bad highway to be on, it can be backed up for miles. Highway 290 goes west from Highway 35 starting a few miles south of Downtown, and Highway 290 goes east from Highway 35 starting a few miles north of Austin. If you are just pulling into town off of 290 heading west from Houston and you turn onto 35 heading south you are going to get a fantastic view of the city.

The on-ramp for Highway 35-S from 290W is a little scary (over 100 feet in the air) but just hold on and look out. You'll see the spotted skyline of Austin and probably will want to have a snack because you may look down and see traffic for miles as well.

Greater Austin is beautiful and slightly complex. There are many things to see and be aware of so let's start with the basics.

Halfway down 35 you will find **Town Lake** and Central **Downtown**. This area is adjacent to the University, **"the Drag"**, **Zilker Park**, and much of what is happening.

Heading west from downtown will get you to US 1 (The Loop, Mopac Expressway). Lake Travis, Westlake, and Bee Caves are some suburbs to the west. Round Rock is to the Northeast.

South Austin (south of Oltorf Street and South Congress Avenue) is a suburb of the rising "Artistic Class" of Austin. Here you will find a lot of your struggling musicians and the people that "Keep Austin Weird."

THE AIRPORT

Austin Airport is easy to get around in, and is currently undergoing construction. They get mad at you if you play on the groovy psychedelic looking piano in the lobby.

AUSTIN AMTRAK STATION

www.texaseagle.com

The Amtrak Station stops just next to Downtown on Lamar Boulevard. You get a complete train travel experience on the **Texas Eagle**, with coaches, sleepers, lounge and a dining car. Direct service to 41 cities between Chicago and L.A., plus 32 other cities via other trains.

THE DRAG

The infamous "Drag" is a must see in Austin. "The Drag" describes an area of decent shopping and food, funky stores, eclectic pedestrians, and interesting stops. It's on Guadalupe Street between 21st and 25th streets.

THE AUSTIN CHRONICLE

www.austinchronicle.com

After landing look around for a local newsstand selling "The Austin Chronicle." The Chronicle has tons of information about ongoing parties, events, music, bars (gay and straight), and some interesting articles. This is a great way to get the local scoop, no matter what your interest is. You'll find detailed reviews on local restaurants, hotels, and entertainment. Also, this paper really is a true reflection of the general mindset of Austin, let's just say that it is more true to the "Keep Austin Weird" philosophy than other publications. This is a great way to get your bearings upon arriving in the Live Music Capital of the World.

The A to Z Listings

Ridiculously Extravagant
Sensible Alternatives
Quality Bargain Spots

24 DINER
600 North Lamar Blvd, Austin, 512-472-5400
www.24diner.com
CUISINE: American/Diner
DRINKS: Full bar
SERVING: 24 hour except Tuesday, closes 1 a.m.;
opens again 6 a.m. Wednesday
PRICE RANGE: $$

Diner concept eatery serving farm-to-table comfort food. Lots of meat dishes and great chili.

ASTI TRATTORIA

408C East 43rd St, Austin, 512-451-1218
www.astiaustin.com/
CUISINE: Italian
DRINKS: Beer & Wine Only
SERVING: Lunch & Dinner; closed Sunday
PRICE RANGE: $$
Popular eatery featuring modern Italian fare including everything from pasta to pizza. Favorites include: Meatballs and the White Pizza. Delicious Tiramisu.

BARLEY SWINE

6555 Burnet Rd, Austin, 512-394-8150
www.barleyswine.com

CUISINE: American (New)
DRINKS: Beer & Wine Only
SERVING: Dinner; open daily, closed Sunday
PRICE RANGE: $$$
The first thing that assaults you when you come in here is the endless variety of jars filled with sauces, pickled veggies, you name it. Seems like there are hundreds of jars everywhere filled with something that you'll be eating tonight. So the place is one big burst of color, color, color. Very friendly and casual. It's a favorite of foodies with a fixed-price tasting menu of seasonal American cuisine. Or you can order a la carte. The food here is so creative, however, that my advice is to go with the tasting menu. You won't regret it. Great dishes like Shishito pepper mousse, Shiitake dumplings, blackened redfish, grilled quail, lamb loin. Delicious desserts. Impressive list of beers.

BLACK SHEEP LODGE
2108 South Lamar Blvd, Austin, 512-707-2744
www.blacksheeplodge.com
CUISINE: Pubs/Burgers
DRINKS: Full Bar
SERVING: Lunch & Dinner; open daily
PRICE RANGE: $$
Sports bar known for its burgers and great daily specials. Impressive list of tap beers and over 125 bottled beers. Favorites include: Black Sheep Chili and Smoked Chipotle Wings.

BUENOS AIRES CAFÉ

1201 East 6th St, Austin, 512-382-1189
www.buenosairescafe.com
CUISINE: Argentine
DRINKS: Beer & Wine Only
SERVING: Lunch & Dinner; open daily, closed for
dinner on Sunday
PRICE RANGE: $$
Artfully decorated café serving an impressive menu
of quality Argentine cuisine. The meats are naturally
raised. Menu includes a variety of tapas, empanadas,
big and small plates. Great ambiance.

CHAMPIONS SPORTS BAR & RESTAURANT

Residence Inn Austin Downtown, 300 East 4th St,
Austin, 512-473-0450
www.hotelaustindowntown.com/dining/champions
CUISINE: Sports Bar/American

DRINKS: Full Bar
SERVING: Breakfast, Lunch & Dinner; open daily
PRICE RANGE: $$
Sports bar with a great menu of comfort food, sandwiches, wraps, tacos, burgers, and salads. 24 televisions, 24 beers on taps. Great place to eat and watch the game.

CHEZ NOUS
510 Neches St, Austin, 512-473-2413
www.cheznousaustin.com
CUISINE: French
DRINKS: Beer & Wine Only
SERVING: Lunch & Dinner during the week, Dinner only on Sat & Sun, closed Mon
PRICE RANGE: $$$
Eatery offering a menu of traditional French fare. Menu picks include: Angus beef and Salmon. Try the chocolate mousse and crème caramel.

CIPOLLINA
1213 West Lynn St, Austin, 512-477-5211
www.cipollina-austin.com
CUISINE: Italian
DRINKS: Beer & Wine Only
SERVING: Lunch & Dinner; open daily
PRICE RANGE: $$
Modern eatery serving a great selection of seasonal Italian fare including homemade pasta, antipasta, pizzas and gourmet paninis.

CLARK'S OYSTER BAR

1200 West 6th St, Austin, 512-297-2525
www.clarksoysterbar.com
CUISINE: Seafood
DRINKS: Full Bar
SERVING: Lunch & Dinner; open daily
PRICE RANGE: $$$
Small neighborhood eatery with a great menu
featuring favorites like lobster rolls, pan roasted
hamburgers, and fresh fish. Raw bar. Nice happy hour
specials. Save room for the delicious chocolate bread
pudding.

CLAY PIT

1601 Guadalupe St., 512-322-5131
www.claypit.com
Clay Pit is a great stop along the way. This menu
boasts nationally acclaimed contemporary Indian
cuisine coupled with an extensive wine menu and
beer (both bottled and draft). Here you can enjoy
another moderately priced night, while enjoying

unleavened bread, goat, rice pudding, deep fried milk pastries and other delicious rarities.

CONTIGO
2027 Anchor Ln, Austin, 512-614-2260
www.contigotexas.com
CUISINE: American Traditional
DRINKS: Full Bar
SERVING: Dinner; Lunch only on Sun
PRICE RANGE: $$
NEIGHBORHOOD: East Austin
Popular eatery that seems "always-packed". Here you can expect family-style seating at picnic tables (most outdoors where there's a fire pit). Menu picks: Dewberry Chicken and Rabbit & Dumplings (delectable) and ox-tongue sliders. Impressive cocktail/wine/beer list.

THE COUNTY LINE
 6500 Bee Cave Rd, Austin, 512-327-1742
www.countyline.com
CUISINE: Barbeque/Steakhouse
DRINKS: Beer & Wine Only
SERVING: Lunch & Dinner; open daily
PRICE RANGE: $$
Popular BBQ eatery serving a menu featuring steaks, fish, and chicken. Vegetarian and gluten-free choices available. Complimentary pumpernickel with every meal but choose the homemade bread – it's heaven.

CURRA'S GRILL

614 E. Oltorf St, 512-444-0012

www.currasgrill.com/

An Austin original, Curra's has excellent cuisine of central Mexico. Some of the best pork recipes around and you will not find better Mexican style seafood dishes anywhere in the city.

DAI DUE

2406 Manor Rd, Austin, 512-524-0688

www.daidue.com

CUISINE: Butcher/American (New)

DRINKS: Beer & Wine Only

SERVING: Lunch, & Dinner; closed Mon

PRICE RANGE: $$

NEIGHBORHOOD: Cherry Wood

Unique eatery serving a menu of creative comfort food with a butcher shop up front that reflects the owner's predilection towards all things MEAT. It started out as a pop-up concept but evolved into this location. Menu favorites include: Smoked pork chop (marinated and rubbed with pepper & honey), wild boar confit, grilled beef ribs, the owner's homemade sausages (I love them—he's a butcher, remember?) Get the biscuits & venison sausages. Many of the dishes prepared in the wood fired grill that is a centerpiece of the room. If you've never had wines from Texas (and who has?), this is a place with a good selection. It's not just the wines that are local, either. Most of the food—from the olive oil to the produce to the meat—comes from less than 200 miles around.

DIPDIPDIP TATSU-YA
7301 Burnet Rd Ste 101, 737-701-6767
www.dipdipdip-tatsuya.com
CUISINE: Japanese
DRINKS: Full Bar
SERVING: Dinner, Closed Mon & Tues.
PRICE RANGE: $$
NEIGHBORHOOD: Crestview
Popular eatery offering a menu of creative Japanese fare. This is a "shabu-shabu" restaurant, which means for you novices out there that you do some of the work preparing your meal. There's a hot pot put in front of you with a boiling broth (you get to choose from 4 types of flavored broths). Then they put the sliced meats next to this and you cook it yourself. There's also the chef-selected omakase menu to choose from if you prefer. Each approach is good. Food is incomparable. The chairs don't have any

backs to them, so you have to sit up, which is a little uncomfortable. But the place is decorated cheerfully with swaths of fabric draped down from the ceiling. Favorites: Wagyu Beef and Meatballs. Great dumplings and sauces. Creative cocktails and nice list of Sakes.

ELIZABETH STREET CAFÉ

1501 S 1st St, Austin, 512-291-2881
www.elizabethstreetcafe.com
CUISINE: Vietnamese/French
DRINKS: Beer & Wine Only
SERVING: Breakfast, Lunch & Dinner; open daily
PRICE RANGE: $$
Cute little eatery that serves a creative menu of Vietnamese and French cuisine. Menu picks include: Short ribs and Kimchi. There's a great soup: chicken & rice with jalapeno & scallions that'll open your eyes. Delicious desserts including éclairs and macaroons.

ENOTECA VESPAIO

1610 Congress Ave S, Austin, 512-441-7672
www.enotecaatx.com/
CUISINE: Italian
DRINKS: Full Bar
SERVING: Lunch & Dinner; open daily
PRICE RANGE: $$
Great place for lunch or Sunday brunch, with a creative menu including Gluten Free items, pizzas, and pastas. For dessert try the Mascarpone Cheesecake or their Tiramisu.

FONDA SAN MIGUEL

2330 W North Loop Blvd, 512-459-4121
www.fondasanmiguel.com
CUISINE: Mexican
DRINKS: Full Bar
SERVING: Dinner nightly, with Lunch only on Sundays
PRICE RANGE: $$
NEIGHBORHOOD: North Loop
Hacienda-style eatery with a bright skylight type ceiling illuminating the Mexican-tiled area below. A nice long bar is off to one side, a great spot to have a margarita before sitting down to dinner. Take special note of the interesting chandeliers hanging from above. There's also quite a bit of original art decorating the walls, a lot of it very good. The dim lighting at night makes the place quite romantic. Serves authentic, upscale Mexican fare. Favorites: Carne asada and Stuffed Chili Rellano. Nice dessert selection.

FOREIGN & DOMESTIC
306 E 53rd St, Austin, 512-459-1010
www.fndaustin.com
CUISINE: American (New)
DRINKS: Beer & Wine Only
SERVING: Dinner; closed Mon; Sunday brunch
PRICE RANGE: $$
NEIGHBORHOOD: Central Austin
Busy eatery offers a creative menu of seasonal American-European fare. If you're in Austin on a Sunday, try to make it to their brunch so you can order the steak and eggs with a hollandaise made with foie gras that I'd never seen before I had it here. Menu picks: Gruyere & Black Pepper Popovers (a favorite) and Crispy Beef Tongue. Menu changes regularly.

FRANKLIN BARBECUE
900 E 11th St, Austin, 512-653-1187
www.franklinbbq.com
CUISINE: Barbecue

DRINKS: Beer & Wine Only
SERVING: Lunch; closed Mondays
PRICE RANGE: $$
NEIGHBORHOOD: East Austin
BBQ fans don't mind standing in line for the incredible "melt-in-your-mouth" brisket and other delicious dishes served here. It started out as a food truck and was so incredibly popular (not just here, but garnering rave press reviews nationwide) that it settled into a small brick-and-mortar location on 11th Street. Note—this is a lunch-only spot and there is always a line – some have been known to wait over five hours but said it was worth it. Chairs are available for those waiting in line and you can buy beer once the place is open. The place attracts repeat customers even with the long line, but these locals know to arrive early to avoid the lines. The smoked turkey, sausages and brisket often sell out by 2 p.m.

FUKUMOTO SUSHI & YAKITORI IZAKAYA
514 Medina St, 512-770-6880
www.fukumotoaustin.com
CUISINE: Sushi Bar/Japanese
DRINKS: Beer & Wine Only
SERVING: Dinner: Closed Sunday
PRICE RANGE: $$$
NEIGHBORHOOD: East Austin
Hip Japanese izakaya offering a menu of skewers, sushi & cooked seafood imported from Japan. Menu picks: Yellow tail Yakitori and Salmon sushi. Another treat is the Bacon wrapped asparagus yakitori.

HABANA RESTAURANT
2728 S Congress Ave, Austin, 512-443-4253
www.habanaaustin.com
CUISINE: Cuban/Caribbean
DRINKS: Full Bar
SERVING: Lunch & Dinner; open daily
PRICE RANGE: $$
If you're a fan of authentic Cuban cuisine then you'll love this place. Great Cuban dishes and tasty mojitos. Outdoor cabanas. Party atmosphere.

HOPFIELDS
3110 Guadalupe St, Austin, 512-537-0467
www.hopfieldsaustin.com
CUISINE: French/Gastropub
DRINKS: Beer & Wine Only
SERVING: Lunch & Dinner; open daily
PRICE RANGE: $$
A gastropub with a French-inspired menu. Great selection of craft beers. Favorites include: French toast burger with grilled onions. Don't leave this place without trying the bread pudding served with house whipped cream.

JEFFREY'S

1204 W Lynn St, Austin, 512-477-5584
www.jeffreysofaustin.com
CUISINE: American
DRINKS: Full Bar
SERVING: Dinner; open daily
PRICE RANGE: $$$$

This upscale fine-dining staple has been the go-to place for special occasions for years. Service includes cocktails made tableside. Favorites include: Steak and Lobster and the cucumber soup. Specials rotate depending on season. Save room for one of their homemade desserts like the old-school baked Alaskan dessert.

JOSEPHINE HOUSE

1601 Waterston Ave, Austin, 512-477-5584
www.josephineofaustin.com
CUISINE: American (Traditional)
DRINKS: Full Bar
SERVING: Lunch, Dinner & Brunch
PRICE RANGE: $$
NEIGHBORHOOD: Clarksville
Set in a charming little cottage – a little annex of the next-door eatery **Jeffrey's**. This place offers an elegant interior with a backyard patio where you can enjoy a relaxing cocktail before you eat. Menu changes often and is printed daily (but on Monday they always serve a delicious and juicy steak frites). Great traditional American fare but with vegetarian options. Great spot for Brunch.

JUAN IN A MILLION

2300 E Cesar Chavez St, Austin, 512-472-3872
www.juaninamillion.com

CUISINE: French
DRINKS: Beer & Wine Only
SERVING: Breakfast, Lunch & Dinner; open daily
PRICE RANGE: $$
Here you'll find traditional Mexican fare including breakfast tacos and authentic Spanish dishes. Inside and outdoor dining.

JUSTINE'S
4710 E 5th St, Austin, 512-385-2900
www.justines1937.com
CUISINE: French
DRINKS: Full Bar
SERVING: Dinner; open daily except Tuesday
PRICE RANGE: $$
This place is pretty and popular so if there are no tables grab a cocktail and sit by the fire pit. The food is worth waiting for. Favorites include: Escargot and Grilled octopus with plantains.

KASBAH
2714 Guadalupe St., 512-289-4752
www.kasbahhookahbar.com
Kasbah is a local favorite. This Moroccan hookah lounge is beautifully constructed. There is seating outside and inside. Inside you'll see other hookah fanatics enjoying premium flavored shishas, chatting with a few friends while listening to transcendental chillout music. This is a great place to socialize and hang out with a few friends. The staff takes great care of their equipment and their customers alike. Kasbah may be a little pricey for your average hookah lounge, but this is not your average hookah lounge.

KEMURI TATSU-YA
2713 E 2nd St, 512-893-5561
www.kemuri-tatsuya.com
CUISINE: Izakaya
DRINKS: Full Bar
SERVING: Dinner, Closed Mon & Tues
PRICE RANGE: $$
NEIGHBORHOOD: East Austin
Casual izakaya serving Japanese and Texan inspired meat-centric dishes. Menu picks: Beef tongue and Marinated jelly fish. Bar scene.

KERBEY LANE
512 477 5717
www.kerbeylanecafe.com

Kerbey Lane is a 24-hour diner with 5 locations in Austin. There is a location on <u>the Drag</u> off of Guadalupe Street in downtown at 2606 Guadalupe St. This one is my personal favorite. The food is amazing and for a decent price. Kerbey lane has a unique menu, featuring the freshest ingredients they can get, a fantastic Tex-Mex breakfast, crazy recipes for pancakes, bottomless coffee, and even sweet potato fries. Kerbey Lane makes an effort to involve itself in the community, working with local vendors, letting artists draw on their walls and supporting local charities. There is a reason that there are five locations in Austin. People love it.

KYOTEN SUSHIKO
4600 Mueller Blvd, 512-666-1287 (TEXT ONLY)
www.kyotensushiko.com
CUISINE: Sushi
DRINKS: Beer &Wine Only
SERVING: Lunch & Dinner; Closed Mon - Wed
PRICE RANGE: $$$$
NEIGHBORHOOD: Austin
Elegant omakase eatery offering an upscale dining experience. Great selection of sushi. Reservations needed. Two seatings of 8 nightly and the chef serves up 18 dishes which are shared.

LA BARBECUE
2401 E Cesar Chavez St, Austin, 512-605-9696
www.labarbecue.com
CUISINE: Barbeque
DRINKS: Beer & Wine Only
SERVING: Wed-Sun 11-6

PRICE RANGE: $$
NEIGHBORHOOD: East Austin
Busy BBQ stand serving a menu including brisket, pulled pork & sausages. Picnic table seating. Go early to avoid the rush or bring your own chairs. Simple dining filled with a crowd of true BBQ fans. (This place gives **Franklin's** some real competition, especially the brisket.)

LA COCINA DE CONSUELO

4516 Burnet Rd, Austin, 512-524-4740
www.consueloskitchen.com
CUISINE: Mexican
DRINKS: No Booze
SERVING: Breakfast, Lunch & Dinner; closed Sat
PRICE RANGE: $
NEIGHBORHOOD: Rosedale
Cozy (and extremely cheap) restaurant set in an old home serving authentic Mexican fare. You really will feel like you're in someone's home. Family atmosphere serving all day. Amazing breakfast tacos, enchiladas and fajitas. BYOB

LA CONDESA

400 W 2nd St, Austin, 512-499-0300
www.lacondesa.com
CUISINE: Mexican
DRINKS: Full Bar
SERVING: Lunch, & Dinner
PRICE RANGE: $$
NEIGHBORHOOD: Downtown / Second Street District
Popular eatery serving Contemporary Mexican dishes. The pastries here are thoroughly unique, not your typical Mexican sweets. The pastry chef here uses herbs, chiles, tropical fruits and corn in startling ways to add a twist to traditional dishes. She even smokes things like chocolate, eggs, cream and butter. Menu favorites include classics like: tacos, ceviches, tostadas, as well as grilled meats and fresh fish. This place boasts the largest premium tequila selection in Austin with over 80 varieties of 100% blue agave tequila. Expect a wait.

LA TRAVIATA
314 N Congress Ave, Austin, 512-479-8131
www.latraviatatx.com
CUISINE: Italian
DRINKS: Full Bar
SERVING: Lunch during the week & Dinner nightly;
closed Sunday.
PRICE RANGE: $$
This intimate, charming trattoria serves a menu of
classic Italian fare. Favorites include the Chicken
parm and Caesar salad. Reservations a must.

LAMBERTS
401 W 2nd St, Austin, 512-494-1500
www.lambertsaustin.com
CUISINE: BBQ
DRINKS: Full Bar
SERVING: Lunch & Dinner; open daily
PRICE RANGE: $$
Definitely a meat-eaters dining establishment with
great BBQ. Favorites include: Beef Brisket and
Smoked Lime Chicken. Creative desserts include:
S'more bread pudding and Vanilla bean flan. Cozy
atmosphere with a nice busy bar upstairs.

LAS TRANCAS TACO STAND
1210 E Cesar Chavez St, Austin, 512) 701-8287
www.facebook.com/Las-Trancas-Taco-Stand-
307145385983596/
CUISINE: Mexican
DRINKS: No Booze
SERVING: Lunch & Dinner; closed Mon

PRICE RANGE: $
NEIGHBORHOOD: East Austin
Possibly the cheapest street tacos you'll find in the city but note that they are some of the best. Small portions so order at least two and you'll be satisfied. All tacos come on two corn tortillas. The only food I do not like is tripe. But here they actually have tripe tacos. They load it up with spices and sauce so you can't taste it, but it's still tripe.

LAUNDERETTE
2115 Holly St, Austin, 512-382-1599
www.launderetteaustin.com
CUISINE: American (New)
DRINKS: Full Bar
SERVING: Lunch & Dinner
PRICE RANGE: $$
NEIGHBORHOOD: East Austin
A converted gas station/laundromat, this hip '50s-style café offers a great menu of American fare. But this is not the same old "comfort food" you expect in a diner. Take the chef's mussels—he prepares the Prince Edward Island mussels in the usual briney broth, but to this he adds not only ground pancetta, but salmi as well. Toss in some Serrano chili butter and Castelvetrano olives and you've got a bowl of mussels you will not soon forget, my friend. Get a side of the homemade olive salad, or take some home with you. It's that good. Other menu picks: Chicken thigh (caramelized chicken) and Crab toast. Creative desserts. Next door what looks like a little mini mart is really a gourmet specialty store, Mister Mc's Grocery Market, that they own. Check it out.

LEFTY'S BRICK BAR
ARRIVE HOTEL
1813-C E 6th St, 737-242-7550
https://www.leftysbrickbar.com/
CUISINE: Seafood/Tapas
DRINKS: Full Bar
SERVING: Lunch & Dinner
PRICE RANGE: $$$
NEIGHBORHOOD: East Austin
Casual indoor/outdoor (picnic tables under umbrellas)
Cajun-style eatery located in a 100-year-old
warehouse that's part of the sleek modern Arrive
Hotel. Favorites: the 'Banh Boy,' which is a hybrid
po' boy and bahn mi stuffed with your choice of pork,
savory chicken, seafood or veggies; Crawfish tail egg
rolls; Red Curry Rotisserie Chicken and Cornmeal
Fried Gulf Shrimp.

LENOIR
1807 S 1st St, Austin, 512-215-9778

www.lenoirrestaurant.com
CUISINE: American (New)
DRINKS: Full Bar
SERVING: Dinner; closed Mon
PRICE RANGE: $$$
NEIGHBORHOOD: Bouldin Creek/South Austin
Tiny eatery offering a rotation 3-course prix fixe menu. Menu picks: Thai fish curry and braised goat roulade. Note: all meats are locally sourced. Impressive wine list. Beautiful romantic setting with chandeliers.

LORO

2115 S Lamar Blvd, 512-916-4858
www.loroaustin.com
CUISINE: Smokehouse/Asian Fusion
DRINKS: Full Bar
SERVING: Lunch & Dinner
PRICE RANGE: $$
NEIGHBORHOOD: South Lamar District
Unique rustic eatery combining Asian smokehouse and Texas barbecue is one of the hottest tickets in town, a "must" for you to visit. Favorites: Malaysian Chicken Bo Ssam and Franklin's brisket, which is smoke for 12 hours before being dressed with fish sauce, Thai chiles and herbs. Here you seat yourself in a very busy dining room. Creative cocktails like the Mango sake slush. Giant patio.

MADAM MAM'S NOODLE

2700 W Anderson Ln, 512-371-9930
www.madammam.com

The menu features Thai Cuisine from Chef Madam Mam. Madam Mam has a history of being a famous chef from Bangkok. Her husband graduated from the University of Texas. After courting for a short while, they got married and opened up this place. This authentic Thai Cuisine can both burn and enlighten your taste buds, all for a reasonable price ($10-$15 for an entrée, $6-$9 for an appetizer).

MAGNOLIA CAFÉ
1920 S Congress Ave, Austin, 512-445-0000
www.themagnoliacafe.com
CUISINE: American (Traditional)/Tex-Mex
DRINKS: Beer & Wine Only
SERVING: 24 hours
PRICE RANGE: $
NEIGHBORHOOD: Bouldin Creek
24-hour Tex-Mex eatery that also offers American "home-cooking." Menu favorites: Gingerbread banana pancakes and the popular Magna Cristo sandwich. Vegan and vegetarian options. Long lines but worth the wait.

MAIKO

311 W 6th St, Austin, 512-236-9888
www.maikoaustin.com
CUISINE: Japanese/Sushi
DRINKS: Full Bar
SERVING: Lunch & Dinner; open daily
PRICE RANGE: $$
This pretty little restaurant offers a creative Japanese menu with Western influences. Menu picks include: Hanger steak and their basic Philadelphia Roll.

MANUEL'S

310 Congress Ave, Austin, 512-472-7555

www.manuels.com
CUISINE: Mexican
DRINKS: Full Bar
SERVING: Lunch & Dinner; open daily
PRICE RANGE: $$
A popular eatery serving traditional Mexican fare.
Favorites include: Manuel's Famous Mole (one of the
best) and the Chile Relleno del Mar. Great Mexican
Mimosas. Gluten-free, dairy free, and vegetarian
options.

MATTIE' S AT GREEN PASTURES
811 West Live Oak St, Austin, 512-444-1888
https://mattiesaustin.com/
CUISINE: French/American
DRINKS: Full Bar
SERVING: Lunch & Dinner; open daily
PRICE RANGE: $$$
Located in a historic Victorian home with a gorgeous
garden with peacocks. Creative menu of French and
American cuisine. Menu favorites include: Pecan
Salmon with Lobster Bread Pudding and Spiced
Spring Rack of Lamb. Definitely try their wonderful
desserts like Chocolate Love – a fat chocolate cake
layered with chocolate mousse.

MAX'S WINE DIVE
207 San Jacinto Blvd, Austin, 512-904-0111
maxswinedive.com
CUISINE: American (New)
DRINKS: Beer & Wine
SERVING: Lunch & Dinner
PRICE RANGE: $$

NEIGHBORHOOD: Downtown
Part of a Texas chain, this popular eatery is known for its comfort food dishes like fried chicken and grilled cheese. Expertly curated selection of wines. Kitchen closed on Mon-Fri from 2 – 4 p.m. and Sat & Sun from 3-4 p.m., but the restaurant is open for wine and beer service.

MELTING POT
13343 Research Blvd, Austin, 512-401-2424
www.meltingpot.com
CUISINE: Fondue/American
DRINKS: Full Bar
SERVING: Lunch weekdays, Dinner nightly.
PRICE RANGE: $$$
This restaurant specializes in Fondue, hence the name, serving heated pots of cheese, chocolate or broth. Try the milk chocolate fondue for a real treat.

MICKLETHWAIT CRAFT MEATS
1309 Rosewood Ave, Austin, 512-791-5961
www.craftmeatsaustin.com
CUISINE: Barbecue
DRINKS: No Booze
SERVING: Lunch, & Dinner; closed Mondays
PRICE RANGE: $$
NEIGHBORHOOD: East Austin
This place is just a trailer with outdoor picnic tables but barbecue fans come in droves. Known for their delicious BBQ meats – particularly the daily smoked-sausage selection and the "insane" beef ribs. Creative menu items like: Pork Shoulder sandwich with Jalapeno Cheese Grits. Homemade breads are great for sopping up the juices. Usually a line but it moves fast.

MOONSHINE PATIO BAR & GRILL
303 Red River St, Austin, 512-236-9599
www.moonshinegrill.com
CUISINE: American/Southern
DRINKS: Full Bar
SERVING: Weekend Brunch, Lunch & Dinner; open daily
PRICE RANGE: $$
Friendly eatery with a contemporary menu of comfort food set in a historic house. Great choice for fans of Southern cuisine. Favorites include: Backyard Chicken sandwich and the Blackened Catfish Platter. Good choice for Sunday brunch.

THE OASIS ON LAKE TRAVIS

6550 Comanche Trail, Austin, 512-266-2442
www.oasis-austin.com
CUISINE: Tex-Mex/Seafood
DRINKS: Full Bar
SERVING: Lunch & Dinner; open daily
PRICE RANGE: $$
Built on a series of terraces, guests love dining on the outdoor decks for the wonder views overlooking Lake Travis. Menu includes Tex-Mex favorites like fajitas and the burgers are pretty good too. Tasty margaritas and a nice selection of beer.

ODD DUCK

1201 S. Lamar Blvd., 512-433-6521
www.oddduckaustin.com
CUISINE: American (Traditional)
DRINKS: Full Bar
SERVING: Dinner
PRICE RANGE: $$$
NEIGHBORHOOD: South Lamar/Bouldin Creek District
Friendly upscale eatery offering locally sourced farm-to-table Southern and TexMex cuisine. Shareable plates, craft beer and cocktails. Popular happy hour. Menu favorites: Redfish Ceviche and Fried Fish Head.

OLAMAIE

1610 San Antonio St, Austin 512-474-2796
www.olamaieaustin.com
CUISINE: Barbecue
DRINKS: Beer & Wine Only
SERVING: Lunch, & Dinner; closed Sun & Mon, dinner only on Tuesday
PRICE RANGE: $$
NEIGHBORHOOD: Downtown
Set in an upscale remodeled home, this is a celebration of Southern fare created by chefs Michael Fojtasek and Grae Nonas. Menu favorites include a delicious Red Snapper and an unforgettable crab salad. Make sure you order the biscuits (an off menu item) and you'll be hooked. Nice wine selection.

OSEYO

1628 E Cesar Chavez St, 512-368-5700
www.oseyoaustin.com
CUISINE: Korean

DRINKS: No Booze
SERVING: Dinner, Closed Mondays
PRICE RANGE: $$
NEIGHBORHOOD: East Austin
Modern eatery offering traditional Korean food.
You'll love the way this simple place is so beautifully
decorated—from the shelves against the wall that
hold things used every day, like plates and glassware,
to the baskets hanging from the ceiling over the
tables. You can eat at the bar, which happens to have
comfortable bar stools with backs on them. (Why are
so many bars offering such crappy stools that are not
comfortable? It's a trend I'm very much against.)
Favorites: Japchae (sweet potato clear noodles stir
fried with veggies); Bulgogi (thin-sliced marinated rib
eye); Ddak Gui (marinated chicken thighs); Pajeon
(Korean scallion pancake). Signature cocktails. Lots
of vegan/vegetarian/gluten-free options.

OTOKO

1603 S Congress Ave, Austin, 512-994-0428
www.otokoaustin.com
CUISINE: Japanese/Sushi Bar
DRINKS: Beer & Wine Only
SERVING: Dinner; closed Sun - Tues
PRICE RANGE: $$$$
NEIGHBORHOOD: South Austin
Usually, when I want to see a show, I go to the
theatre. Now, you can go to restaurants instead! An
exclusive 12-seat eatery by James Beard Foundation
Award-winner Paul Qui. Dining here is a unique
experience from a tasting menu that blends Tokyo-
style sushi with Kyoto-style kaiseki. Guests can

watch (and watch and watch and watch, as they take their good sweet time about it) the food being prepared and even interact with the chefs. The fish is flown in twice a week in order to guarantee freshness.

PATRIZI'S

2307 Manor Rd, Austin, 512-522-4834
www.patrizis.com
CUISINE: Italian/Food Stands
DRINKS: Beer & Wine Only
SERVING: Dinner
PRICE RANGE: $$
NEIGHBORHOOD: East Austin
Located outside the Vortex theater, this food truck offers a menu of Italian standards and homemade pastas made daily. Menu favorites: Bacon carbonara. Once a month they offer a Wednesday dinner night offering a special menu. Dining is outside.

THE PEACHED TORTILLA

5520 Burnet Rd #100, 512-330-4439
www.thepeachedtortilla.com
CUISINE: Asian Fusion, Southern
DRINKS: Full Bar
SERVING: Dinner, Lunch on Fri, Sat, & Sun, Closed Mondays
PRICE RANGE: $$$
NEIGHBORHOOD: Allandale
Casual eatery that does something you don't see every day—mixing Asian food (and techniques) with Southern comfort food. Results are very agreeable, I'm glad to say. Favorites: BBQ Brisket Taco; Thai

Chopped Salad; Vietnamese Pork Chop; and Hanger Steak. Extensive whiskey menu.

PERLA'S
1400 S Congress Ave, Austin, 512-291-7300
www.perlasaustin.com
CUISINE: Seafood
DRINKS: Full Bar
SERVING: Lunch & Dinner; open daily
PRICE RANGE: $$$
Great place for patio dining and features and open kitchen. Menu favorites are the fish, surf 'n' turf and oysters. Great brunch choice. Breakfast favorites include: Breakfast crab cake and the Big Blue Banana & Bacon pancake.

PERRY'S STEAKHOUSE & GRILLE
114 W 7th St, Austin, 512-474-6300
www.perryssteakhouse.com
CUISINE: Steakhouse/Seafood
DRINKS: Full Bar
SERVING: Dinner; open daily
PRICE RANGE: $$$
Upscale eatery with a lounge. Favorite dishes: Fried calamari and Tuna tartar. Nice bar with live music.

ROARING FORK
701 Congress Ave, Austin, 512-583-0000
www.roaringfork.com
CUISINE: American
DRINKS: Full Bar
SERVING: Lunch weekdays, Dinner nightly
PRICE RANGE: $$

Located in downtown, this charming eatery offers a nice dining experience. The menu include great open flame grilled steaks and fish, and oven-baked flatbreads. Nice wine list and craft brews.

SALT AND TIME

1912 E. Seventh St., Austin, 512-524-1383
www.saltandtime.com
CUISINE: American (New)
DRINKS: Beer & Wine
SERVING: Lunch & Dinner; Sunday brunch
PRICE RANGE: $$
NEIGHBORHOOD: East Austin
Rustic eatery located in a butcher shop with a menu of farm-to-table American fare. Extensive beer list and adequate wine list. Interesting meat selections like salami, flaxen rib, and pork belly.

THE SALT LICK BBQ

3350 Palm Valley Blvd., Round Rock, 512-386-1044

www.saltlickbbq.com/
Though it's a few miles outside of Austin, it's well worth a drive to eat the BBQ here. They offer a family special that's really hard to beat: all you can eat beef brisket, sausage, pork ribs, potato salad, cole slaw and beans. Bread, pickles and onions on request. $19.95 per person. (Kids cheaper.)

SCHOLZ GARTEN
1607 San Jacinto Blvd., 512-474-1958
www.scholzgarten.com
The oldest continuously operating restaurant and also the oldest business in Texas, launched in the great year 1866, right after the Civil War. Good German and other hearty fare. (I come here for the Beef Stroganoff—it's a special on Tuesday for only $7.50.) As the name implies, Scholz Garten also has a biergarten and serves many different types of beer. A traditional Democratic party hangout where Ann Richards is supposed to have plotted her successful run for governor. In the middle of it all, the Capitol is a few blocks away and the University of Texas is just north.

SIXTH AND WALLER
EAST AUSTIN HOTEL
1108 E 6th St, Austin, 737-205-8888
www.eastaustinhotel.com
CUISINE: Breakfast, Sandwiches
DRINKS: Full Bar
SERVING: Breakfast, Lunch, & Dinner
PRICE RANGE: $$
NEIGHBORHOOD: East Austin

Simple diner-style eatery located in the trendy East Austin Hotel. Has those circular diner stools along the counter, or sit in one of the tables scattered about in this bright and cheerful room with some tables topped off with colorful tiles. Lots of healthy options. Favorites: Burrata Salad and Pastrami sandwich.

STILES SWITCH BBQ

6610 N Lamar Blvd, Austin, 512-380-9199
www.stilesswitchbbq.com
CUISINE: Barbeque
DRINKS: Beer & Wine Only
SERVING: Lunch & Dinner; closed Mon
PRICE RANGE: $$
NEIGHBORHOOD: Brentwood
Located in Violet Crown shopping center, this popular BBQ joint "real" central Texas BBQ. Menu favorites: Brisket, turkey and sausage – all worth the trip. Craft beer on draft.

STUBB'S BBQ

801 Red River St, Austin, 512-480-8341
www.stubbsaustin.com
CUISINE: Barbecue
DRINKS: Full Bar
SERVING: Lunch, & Dinner, Sunday Brunch
PRICE RANGE: $$
NEIGHBORHOOD: Downtown / Red River District
Located in a historic 1850s building but nobody comes here for a history lesson—they come for the delicious Texas barbecue or the acts performing on stage (the amphitheater has welcomed acts like Willie Nelson, Bob Dylan and James Brown). Menu

favorites include: the brisket and ribs. Serving BBQ since 1968.

SWIFT'S ATTIC
315 Congress Ave, Austin, 512-482-8842
www.swiftsattic.com
CUISINE: American (New)/Gastropub
DRINKS: Full Bar
SERVING: Lunch, & Dinner, Sunday Brunch; Dinner only on Saturdays
PRICE RANGE: $$
NEIGHBORHOOD: Downtown
Popular, retro-chic eatery offering a menu of creative small plates. Their bar attracts singles and couples in equal measure in a comfortable atmosphere. The late-night menu is particularly good. Vegetarian options. Great choice for Sunday brunch. Bar serves tasty craft cocktails and a nice wine list.

TAKOBA
1411 E 7th St, Austin, 512-628-4466

www.takobarestaurant.com
CUISINE: Mexican
DRINKS: Full Bar
SERVING: Lunch & Dinner; open daily
PRICE RANGE: $$
This trendy eatery serves Mexican standards with a great Mezcal bar known for creative cocktails. This place has the best guacamole and the Chicken Mole enchilada is tasty too.

THE TAVERN
922 W 12th St, Austin, 512-320-8377
www.tavernaustin.com
CUISINE: American
DRINKS: Full Bar
SERVING: Lunch & Dinner; open daily
PRICE RANGE: $$
A very popular sports bar with 50 high-def TVs and a rotating beer menu. Great bar grub like the Cheddar Blanket burger and the Queso burger. Upstairs patio.

TLV – Israeli Street Food
111 Congress Ave, Fairground #7, 512-608-4041
www.tlv-austin.com
CUISINE: Middle Easter / Israeli
DRINKS: Full Bar
SERVING: Breakfast, Lunch, & Dinner
PRICE RANGE: $$$
NEIGHBORHOOD: Downtown
Israeli street food served on plates or in Pita with very basic, no-frills counter service in a modern setting. Favorites: Chicken with hummus & pita bread and

Eggplant-based hummus bowl topped with added falafel. Tahini shakes. Creative desserts.

TRACE
W Austin, 200 Lavaca St, Austin, 512-542-3660
www.traceaustin.com
CUISINE: American
DRINKS: Full Bar
SERVING: Breakfast, Lunch & Dinner; open daily
PRICE RANGE: $$$
A sophisticated eatery offering a seasonal menu typical of Central Texas that makes foodies drool. Favorites include: Seared Tuna with celery curls and tiny grape slivers and Pork Five Ways. Very creative specials that keep the customers returning.

TRULUCK'S
Great Hills Station, 10225 Research Blvd, Austin, 512-794-8300
www.trulucks.com
CUISINE: Seafood/Steakhouse
DRINKS: Full Bar
SERVING: Dinner; open daily
PRICE RANGE: $$$
This is a great place for foodies or anyone who just appreciates a great meal. Favorites include: miso-glazed sea bass and the succulent crab. Their carrot cake is one of the best. Impressive wine list.

UCHI

801 S Lamar Blvd, Austin, 512-916-4808
www.uchiaustin.com
CUISINE: Japanese/Sushi
DRINKS: Beer & Wine Only
SERVING: Dinner; open daily
PRICE RANGE: $$$$
Chef Tyson Cole offers a creative menu of Sushi and contemporary Japanese fare. Try the tasting menus for a great dining experience.

UCHIKO

4200 N Lamar Blvd, Austin, 512-916-4808
www.uchikoaustin.com
CUISINE: Sushi/Japanese
DRINKS: Beer & Wine Only
SERVING: Dinner
PRICE RANGE: $$$$
NEIGHBORHOOD: Rosedale
Gluten-free options

Here you'll be treated to the creations of renowned executive chef and James Beard Award winner Tyson Cole, a Japanese-speaking white guy who serves up the best sushi in Austin. Menu picks include: Yellowtail Chili (duck, Brussels Sprouts and Pork Belly); mackerel with potato-milk jam & green apple; smoked bonito with watermelon radish; We actually ordered about 12 items and everyone shared and everything that I tried was amazing. Nice selection of wine and sake.

URBAN AN AMERICAN GRILL

The Westin Austin at The Domain, 11301 Domain Dr, Austin, 512-490-1511
www.urbanatthedomain.com
CUISINE: American
DRINKS: Full Bar
SERVING: Dinner; open daily
PRICE RANGE: $$
Located at Westin at the Domain, this relaxed eatery offers a creative menu of comfort food. Favorites include Seared Ahi salad and Rib eye with caramelized Brussels sprouts.

UROKO

1023 Springdale Rd Bldg 1 Suite C, 512-520-4004
www.urokoaustin.com
CUISINE: Japanese
DRINKS: Wine, Beer & Sake
SERVING: Lunch & Dinner, Closed Sundays
PRICE RANGE: $$$
NEIGHBORHOOD: East Austin

Almost devoid of any décor at all, this place features Tamaki (Sushi hand roll) with a chef-selected menu of fatty salmon, fatty hamachi, unagi, spicy tuna and salmon skin. Sushi classes available. They offer 3 difference experiences: the counter service offering Tamaki, room for sushi classes, and the 45-minute sushi omakase but this is only on the weekends.

VALENTINA'S TEX MEX BBQ
11500 Manchaca Rd, 512-221-4248
www.valentinastexmexbbq.com
CUISINE: Food Truck/Barbeque/Tex-Mex

DRINKS: No Booze
SERVING: Breakfast (from 7:30), Lunch, & Dinner till 9 (or till they sell out of BBQ for the day); Closed Tuesday
PRICE RANGE: $
NEIGHBORHOOD: Austin
Set in a trailer, this wonderful food truck offers a menu of mesquite-smoked BBQ with a Tex-Mex Twist. Here you choose from a traditional BBQ sandwich on buns or BBQ taco on flour tortillas (which I like far better). The brisket is rubbed with cayenne & garlic. Tomato-serrano salsa is excellent. Picks: Pork ribs and Pork tip taco special. They offer a big open-air shed in which they have some picnic tables and you can eat in there or outside. I will have to admit that they've thought of every convenience—there are even a couple of Port a Potties where you can relieve yourself. (In all my worldwide travels, I've never been to a "restaurant" that offered *this* to its customers.) If there's a line, do not let that dissuade you—this food is worth it.

VAMONOS
4807 Airport Blvd, Austin, 512-474-2029
www.vamonos-texmex.com
CUISINE: Tex-Mex
DRINKS: Full Bar
SERVING: Lunch & Dinner, Closed Sundays
PRICE RANGE: $$
NEIGHBORHOOD: Hyde Park
The eye-popping bright blue chairs make this popular Tex-Mex eatery stand out when you walk inside. Otherwise, it's pretty much no frills. But you're here

for the food. Favorites: Carnitas tacos; Chicken enchiladas verde; Tacos with grilled redfish. Free chips and salsa. Family friendly. Impressive list of tequilas.

VAQUERO TAQUERO
Restaurant: 104 E 31st St, 512-366-5578
www.vaquerotaquero.com
CUISINE: Tacos/Food Truck
DRINKS: No Booze
SERVING: **Restaurant** serves 7-11 & 5-9 Tues-Fri; on weekends, 9:30 to 2.
PRICE RANGE: $
NEIGHBORHOOD: Hyde Park
This eatery is all about the taco, and you get 4 options: Chicken, steak, veggie or pork. Freshly made with homemade flour and corn tortillas. Simply scrumptious. Also serves breakfast.

VERACRUZ ALL NATURAL

1704 E Cesar Chavez St, Austin, 512-981-1760
www.veracruztacos.com
CUISINE: Mexican/Food Truck
DRINKS: No Booze
SERVING: Breakfast/Lunch
PRICE RANGE: $
NEIGHBORHOOD: East Austin
Authentic Mexican fare served from a trailer with
picnic tables for seating. Everything is made with
fresh ingredients with homemade tortillas and chips.
And trust me, this makes a difference. Picks:
breakfast tacos (have you ever had a breakfast
taco?—try it—you'll love them) and homemade mole
tacos. They have a tilapia taco made with a seasoning
so good you'll forget it's tilapia. On weekends only,
they serve up their barbacoa taco, with a secret sauce

that makes it a special taco indeed. Nice selection of fresh juices and smoothies.

VESPAIO
1610 S Congress Ave, Austin, 512-441-6100
www.austinvespaio.com
CUISINE: Italian
DRINKS: Full Bar
SERVING: Dinner; open daily
PRICE RANGE: $$$
Popular eatery offering an intimate dining experience. Menu picks include: Pumpkin ravioli and Lasagna. Great selection of fresh pasta, breads and deserts. Wine list features most small boutique brands.

VIXEN'S WEDDING
ARRIVE HOTEL
1813 E 6th St, 737-242-7555
www.vixensweddingatx.com
CUISINE: Indian/Portuguese
DRINKS: Full Bar
SERVING: Dinner
PRICE RANGE: $$
NEIGHBORHOOD: East Austin
An Indian and Portuguese-inspired eatery serving family style food served in a cheerful and lively atmosphere with bright colors everywhere. Favorites: Pork Ribs Vindaloo; Chaat fried okra; and Black spiced lamb. Creative cocktails. Daily Happy hour.

WINK
1014 N Lamar Blvd, Austin, 512-482-8868
www.winkrestaurant.com

CUISINE: American/Vegetarian
DRINKS: Beer & Wine Only
SERVING: Dinner; nightly except Sunday
PRICE RANGE: $$
A favorite Austin eatery that features a great chef's tasting menu that is updated daily. Feature a daily Vegetarian tasting menu. Favorites include: House cured salmon and the Hangar steak. Great wine pairings.

THE YARD MILKSHAKE BAR
3400 Esperanza Crossing, 512-551-9542
www.theyardmilkshakebar.com/austin
CUISINE: Desserts
DRINKS: No Booze
SERVING: Open noon – 10 p.m.
PRICE RANGE: $$
NEIGHBORHOOD: North Burnett
A casual milkshake bar that serves indulgent ice cream creations. 3 menus offered so mark your choices before you step up to the counter. Also available—bowls, cones, floats, waffles, and doughnuts. Expect large portions.

<u>NIGHTLIFE</u>

ALAMO DRAFTHOUSE CINEMA
2700 W Anderson Lane, Austin, 512-861-7030
www.drafthouse.com
NEIGHBORHOOD: Downtown / Sixth Street
District
What a great idea to mix beer, movies and great food
all under one roof. Great selection of films shown
without commercials. No need to run around – one
stop for dinner and a movie.

BANGER'S SAUSAGE HOUSE & BEER GARDEN
79 Rainey St, Austin, 512-386-1656
www.bangersaustin.com

NEIGHBORHOOD: Downtown / Sixth Street
District
Known for their homemade sausages (over 30 styles
made in-house) and draft beer selection – over 10
beers on draft and another 50 in cans and bottles. Live
music, a dog park, and lots of fun, especially if you're
younger than I am, LOL. They have those beer hall
style benches for seating. Great place for brunch.
Sixth Street is a great place for a bar crawl, because
there are so many of them populated by the students
in Austin. This is a good place to indoctrinate
yourself to Sixth Street.

BLUE OWL BREWING
2400 East Cesar Chavez, 512-593-1262
www.blueowlbrewing.com
Known for their sour-mashed beers but unfortunately,
their liquor license doesn't allow them to sell their
beer. So, you have to buy a glass ($14) and they will
fill it complimentary. Favorite sours: Professor Black
Cherry Stout, Admiral Gravitas Imperial Stout and
Hop Totem IPA.

THE BROKEN SPOKE
3201 S Lamar Blvd, Austin, 512-442-6189
www.brokenspokeaustintx.net
NEIGHBORHOOD: South Austin
If you're looking for an authentic Texas honky-tonk
experience, this is the place. They even offer free line
dance classes on some nights. This place is an
institution. Lots of cold beer, excellent bar food and
honest-to-God country music.

BUNGALOW

92 Rainey St., 512-363-5475

www.facebook.com/bungalowatx/

Cute little bar featuring a variety of local beers on tap.
One of those friendly bars where everybody knows
your name. Happy hour specials, sports, music,
outdoor patio with games and a taco truck.

CACTUS CAFE

2247 Guadalupe St. (inside Texas Union Building at
24th), 512-475-6515

https://cactuscafe.org/

Weekdays, 11a.m. to 7p.m. (later if there's a
performance). Happy hour 4-7; Saturday, 8p.m. to
midnight; closed Sunday. Shows begin at 8:30, with
ticket sales beginning 30 minutes before showtime.
Along **the Drag** you'll find this great Live music
venue with full bar. Tickets sold on a first-come, first-
served basis. Cactus has acquired a national
reputation, showcasing the top local, regional,
national and international acoustic music acts on the
circuit today. Billboard magazine listed the Cactus as
one of 15 "solidly respected, savvy clubs" nationwide
"from which careers can be cut, that work with
proven names and new faces."

CONTAINER BAR

90 Rainey St, 512-320-0820

www.austincontainerbar.com

Here the entire bar is made from old shipping
containers (hence the name) but this place packs them
in. Great beer selection, DJs, and there's even a food
truck inside if you get hungry.

THE CONTINENTAL CLUB
1315 S. Congress, 512-441-2444
www.continentalclub.com
This legendary South Austin venue was opened in
1957 and for nearly four decades has been serving up
the best live music Austin has to offer. The venue is
small so get there early if you want to get in.

ELEPHANT ROOM
315 Congress Ave., 512-473-2279
www.elephantroom.com
Weekdays (from 4p.m. to 2a.m.) usually no cover
charge. Weekends (from 8p.m. to 2 a.m.) a small
cover.
Downtown in the Warehouse District is this great spot
for jazz and blues. Live music every night, even
during happy hour (4-8, music from 6-8). This place
gives off an authentic Austin vibe.

EMO'S
Emo's East, 2015 E. Riverside, 888-512-7469

www.emosaustin.com/
Emo's is an interesting place to catch a live show.
You'll catch local and some not-so-local artists and
bands rocking out here. The bands that come through
range anywhere from punk rockabilly, to 80s
Depeche-Mode sounds.

HANDLEBAR

121 E. 5th St., Austin, 512-344-9571
www.handlebaraustin.com/
NEIGHBORHOOD: Downtown
Austin's only moustache bar featuring an outdoor
deck with games, a photo booth, and bartenders
sporting handlebar moustaches. Craft cocktails.

JAVELINA

69 Rainey St, 512-382-6917
www.javelinabar.com
Casual bar with an outdoor patio. Bar serves creative
cocktails and draft beers and offers a menu of Texan
fare like Fried chicken and Cobb salad.

JESTER KING BREWERY

13187 Fitzhugh Rd, 512-661-8736
www.jesterkingbrewery.com
Popular brewery that offers a tasting room and
extensive beer list featuring wild ales and locally
fermented beers. The venue includes the brewery,
Stanley's Farmhouse Pizza and a communal area for
dining and drinking. Free brewery tours.

HALF STEP

75 1/2 Rainey Street, Austin, 512-589-2716

NEIGHBORHOOD: East Austin
A non-assuming but swanky lounge in the heart of the Rainey Street nightlife district offering a short menu of crafted cocktails. The cocktails served lean toward classics and creative mixtures, like the Cider Julip, concocted from Eastsiders Original Dry Cider (made here in Austin) mint leaves, bitters and Domaine Dupont Calvados. Yum. This bar boasts the only Clinebell ice machine in town and a private-party room. Out back on the patio there's a ping pong table and you're welcome to play.

MEZCALERIA TOBALA

1816 E 6th St, Austin, 512-480-0781

NEIGHBORHOOD: East Austin
Located in a rustic space above **Whisler's**, this Mezcal-themed bar serves brand name libations and traditional bar snacks. They even serve the drinks in the appropriate vessel: *copitas* made of red clay. For those looking for an Oaxacan-style mezcaleria, this place serves a variety of mezcals including Mexicano, Madre Cuixe, and some rare Espandin.

MIDNIGHT COWBOY

313 E 6th St, Austin, 512-843-2715

NEIGHBORHOOD: Downtown
This intimate lounge features a speakeasy atmosphere (no sign – just a plain black door, very fitting given the rambunctious nature of Sixth Street—this place once was a brothel). This old-school bar serves

vintage cocktails to classy upscale crowd. They prefer reservations, but if you see the "vacant" sign lighted up, it means they will take you as a walk-in.

PÉCHÉ
208 W 4th St., 512-494-4011
www.pecheaustin.com
In the Warehouse District in Downtown you'll find this upscale lounge with brick-lined walls, high wood-beamed ceiling, and a back bar as good as any in the country. Knowledgeable mixologists behind this bar. Has a nice bar menu: beef Carpaccio, salt cod Arancini (always a winner here), pan-fried oysters, steak frites, and a pork T-bone, a cut you don't see very often.

RAINEY STREET
raineystbars.com

Formerly a residential area, this street now is the address of some of Austin's top restaurants and bars. Rainey Street Historic District also features a selection of historic homes – many now converted into bars or restaurants.

REVOLUTION SPIRITS DISTILLERY
12345 Paul's Valley Rd, 512-358-1203
www.revolutionspirits.com
Open only on Saturdays. Known for their award-winning liquor and signature Austin Reserve Gin. This place is small but the selection is huge offering everything from fruit liquors to the flagship gin to Cafecito coffee liqueurs. Tour available but just walk in and start tasting.

ROOSEVELT ROOM
307 W 5th St, 512-494-4094
www.therooseveltroomatx.com
Industrial space with an upstairs lounge offering an impressive menu of classic and crafted cocktails. Try the Cigar Box – a cocktail that comes with a lit cinnamon stick that looks like a cigar. Reservations recommended.

SPEAKEASY

412 Congress Ave, Austin, 512-476-8017
www.speakeasyaustin.com
NEIGHBORHOOD: Downtown / Warehouse District
Located in the Warehouse District, this multilevel
nightclub features live music nightly and live DJs on
the weekend. Great place for dancing. Rooftop lounge
with great view of downtown Austin.

WHIP IN

1950 SI-35, Austin, 512-442-5337
www.whipin.com
NEIGHBORHOOD: South Austin

Convenience store / café that's situated in an old
Singer Sewing Machine factory attracts crowds not
only for its funky atmosphere, but for its large beer
selection. It's really kind of a mish mash of
experiences: beer hall (they sport 50 taps, one of them
Whip In's own line of beer), wine bar and a restaurant
featuring a menu of Indian cuisine mixed with Tex-
Mex, if you can imagine such a thing. Queso with
chutney, goast sliders, Asian Frito Pie. Different,
right? Whatever. It's a lot of fun here. Outdoor patio
and live music nightly around 9.

WHISLER'S
1816 E 6th St, Austin, 512-480-0781
www.whislersatx.com
NEIGHBORHOOD: East Austin
Chic watering hole serving handcrafted cocktails.
Busy happy hour scene with drink specials. Outdoor
patio and frequent live music. One of the more
interesting places in Austin. There's a tequila bar up
the stairs you won't want to miss.

INDEX

O

P

R

S

T

U

www.ingramcontent.com/pod-product-compliance
Ingram Content Group UK Ltd.
Pitfield, Milton Keynes, MK11 3LW, UK
UKHW021646190726
13853UKWH00001B/76